63rd (R.N.)

TRENCH STANDING

ORDERS.

(2nd Edition)

LONDON:

PRINTED UNDER THE AUTHORITY OF HIS MAJESTY'S STATIONERY OFFICE
BY HARRISON AND SONS, 45–47, ST. MARTIN'S LANE, W.C.,
PRINTERS IN ORDINARY TO HIS MAJESTY.

1917.

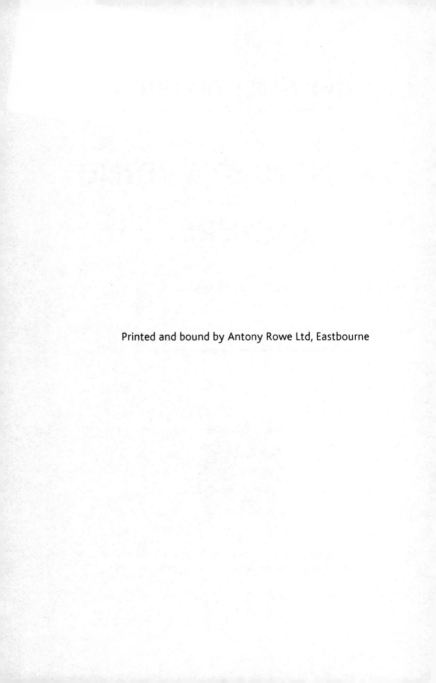

Printed and bound by Antony Rowe Ltd, Eastbourne

CONTENTS.

PART I.

TAKING OVER AND HANDING OVER TRENCHES.

PART II.

TRENCH ROUTINE.

PART III.

WORK ON TRENCHES.

PART IV

ACTION IN CASE OF ATTACK.

PART V

PRECAUTIONS AGAINST GAS.

PART VI.

COMMUNICATIONS.

APPENDICES.

APPENDIX I.

APPENDIX II.

APPENDIX III.

63rd (R.N.) DIVISION
TRENCH STANDING ORDERS.

PART I.—TAKING OVER AND HANDING OVER TRENCHES.

1.—RELIEFS.

1. When a battalion takes over a new line of trenches, the battalion commander, the adjutant, company commanders, one junior officer and one non-commissioned officer from each company, and one man from each platoon, will visit the trenches on the day previous to the relief. They will gain as much information as possible from the battalion they are relieving, and will pay particular attention to the following points :— *Preliminary reconnaissance.*

    (a) Number of men holding line to be taken over, and their distribution.
    (b) Dug-out and shelter accommodation.
    (c) Work in hand and proposed.
    (d) Condition of wire and defences generally.
    (e) Water supply.
    (f) Communications.
    (g) Artillery support.
    (h) Information as to the enemy, his habits, snipers, machine gun and trench mortar positions, the work he is doing, &c.
    (i) Dangerous points

The junior officers, N.C.Os. and men alluded to above will remain in the line and await the arrival of their companies. The men must know their way about the trenches and be able to act as orderlies by the time their companies arrive.

Officers proceeding to the line previous to taking over will invariably report to the H.Q. of the unit in the line, both on arrival and departure.

2. An officer of each company will proceed in advance to the trenches on the day of relief to take over during daylight all trench stores, ammunition, &c. (*see* Sec. **2, 4**). Mutual receipts for these will be signed.

A list of articles included in the term " trench stores " is given in Appendix I.

Specialists
3. Lewis gunners, observers, snipers, and a proportion of signallers will, as a rule, not be relieved on the same day as companies. They should proceed to the trenches 24 hours before their battalions, and take over their posts during daylight.

M.G. Cos.
4. Machine gun companies will be relieved 24 hours after the infantry.

Guides.
5. Arrangements will be made between the commanding officers of relieving and about-to-be-relieved battalions as to places where guides will meet the former to conduct them to the trenches.

At least one guide per platoon, machine gun, or special post, and one for each company headquarters will be provided.

Guides must know the exact spot at which they are to meet relieving troops, and the best and safest route to the trenches.

March discipline.
6. The strictest march discipline will be maintained by all parties proceeding to or from the trenches. An officer will march in rear of each company to ensure that it is properly closed up. This especially applies to taking over a new line, when a slow rate of progress is essential, so that all may keep touch.

Reliefs will be carried out as quietly as possible. No smoking or lights will be allowed after reaching a point to be decided on by the battalion commander.

Action in case of attack.
7. Before commencing a relief every party must receive orders as to what action it will take in the event of an attack or an alarm while the relief is in progress. As a general principle any retirement of troops will be avoided. Troops caught in the open during a relief will, as a general rule, occupy the nearest trench or cover available, and get into touch at once with the nearest troops holding the trench line.

Bombers will carry bombs detonated and ready for use.

8. As far as circumstances permit, and whenever there is a probability of attack, reliefs will be carried out gradually, so that large numbers of men are not moving in the open at the same time.

2.—TAKING OVER TRENCHES.

The platoon commander.
1. The platoon will file in and occupy the section of trench it is to hold. The platoon commander will at once post sentries in relief of those in the line while the remainder of the platoon stands to arms. He will satisfy himself that each sentry and listening post is properly relieved, and that the orders for the post are correctly handed over. The greatest care and attention to detail are necessary in this.

The platoon commander will then personally examine all firing positions, and satisfy himself that each man can fire at the foot of the nearest part of our own wire. He will inspect the position of his Lewis gun and ensure that the orders for the gun are understood.

He will obtain from the troops relieved all the latest information regarding the trench, the hostile trenches, &c., and is responsible for taking over all tools and other trench stores in the trench. He will personally visit the platoon commanders on either side of him, and will ascertain the position of the water supply, the platoon latrines, the company telephone, company headquarters, and the nearest supporting troops, and will arrange that his orderlies become thoroughly acquainted with all routes to company and battalion headquarters. He will examine the ammunition and bomb magazines and anti-gas stores.

As soon as he has satisfied himself on all the above points he will report relief complete to his company commander.

2. On taking over a line of trenches the company commander will generally supervise the taking over by his platoons. He will obtain from the unit relieved all the latest information regarding the line, work in progress, &c., and will take over the log-book, written up to date, and such trench maps as are available. He will get in touch with the companies on his right and left. He will ascertain the position of the nearest supporting troops, of the reserve ammunition, of his Lewis guns and of any machine guns, or special posts in his line, and the position of his battalion headquarters. He will ascertain the best and quickest means of obtaining artillery support, and will have all wires tested, including the wire to the artillery. As soon as his platoon commanders have reported that they have taken over, and he is satisfied that all is correct, he will inform his battalion commander that his company has completed the relief. *The company commander.*

The company will not be dismissed until all the platoon commanders have reported that everything is in order.

As soon as possible after taking over a new line, company commanders will, if the tactical situation permits, forward to the battalion commander a report on each of the trenches for which they are responsible, with the following information :—

> Garrison of trench.
> Field of fire.
> Distance from enemy's trench.
> General condition of trench.
> Number and position of sniper's posts.
> Whether he has sufficient gas gongs, &c.
> Whether every man has a post from which he can see and bring fire to bear on the foot of our own wire.
> Thickness and height of parapets.
> Whether there are sufficient traverses.
> State of our own wire, giving approximate width.
> State of enemy's wire.

A rough sketch with all details should accompany this report, also a statement showing proposed work, and a list of ammunition, tools, and trench stores taken over.

The
battalion
head-
quarters.

3. A battalion taking over a line of trenches will similarly obtain from the battalion which it relieves all latest available information regarding the line, work in hand and proposed, the position of neighbouring units, the S.A.A. and trench stores available, and a copy of the defence scheme. All the latest information about the enemy and his trenches and activities will also be obtained, together with a large scale map of No Man's Land corrected to date, and such trench maps as are available.

Trench
stores.

4. As soon as possible after taking over a line, copies of receipts for trench and R.E. stores taken over will be sent to brigade headquarters on the authorised form. Copies of these receipts will in turn be forwarded to divisional headquarters by brigades.

Battalion entrenching tools will not be taken to the trenches. Should the supply of tools on charge as " trench stores " be insufficient brigades will draw such tools as are necessary from the R.E.

3.—HANDING OVER TRENCHES.

1. Officers handing over trenches are responsible that all available information and trench maps of the locality are given to the relieving troops, and that all tools and trench stores (as enumerated on the authorised form) are collected and handed over in the most convenient way and place. Receipts must be obtained for everything handed over, and must be forwarded to brigade headquarters.

The following will not be handed over :—

> Very pistols.
> Pistols, illuminating, 1½-in.
> Telescopic rifles.
> Telephones.
> Periscopes.

A supply of Very lights and other consumable stores, sufficient for at least 24 hours, should be handed over to the relieving unit.

2. Great care must be taken that all orders relative to the line which have been received by companies, battalions, or brigade during their tour of duty are handed over to the relieving units. They should also be entered in the log-books.

3. Whenever possible, reports on trenches, similar to the report described in the last paragraph of Sec. 2, 2, will be prepared and handed over to relieving units on the day previous to the relief taking place. Log-books, entered up to date, will be handed over on the day of relief.

4 The troops being relieved will not leave the trenches until :—

(a) All trench stores have been handed over, and receipts received.

(b) The relieving troops are in position and sentries posted.

(c) Orders to move have been received from the company commander.

PART II.—TRENCH ROUTINE.

4 —GARRISON OF TRENCHES.

1. During daylight the front line trenches should be held as lightly as is compatible with safety, the defences being entrusted mainly to Lewis guns. At night the garrison must be strengthened.

2. The actual strength of garrisons will be governed by the tactical situation, and by the number of support and communication trenches.

5.—DUTIES.

1. One officer in each company and one N.C.O. in each platoon will always be on duty. When a company has only two officers, the sergeant-major or N.C.O's commanding platoons may be included in the duty officers' roster.

Numbers required and length of tour.

2. The length of each tour of duty will depend on the number of officers and N.C.Os. in each company and on the weather. Normally each tour should be, by day 4 hours, by night 2 hours, day commencing at " morning stand to " and night at " evening stand to." In inclement weather the length of a tour of duty must be reduced.

3. By night the officer on duty will visit each sentry and listening post found by his company at least once during his tour. He will also supervise the work of the company working parties. He will be responsible for sending in the reports required by battalion head-quarters unless there is anything unusual to report, when this duty will be performed by the company commander. He will carry a Very pistol and a few cartridges. At the end of his tour he will call the next officer for duty and hand over to him.

Special duties by night.

4. N.C.O.s on duty at night will frequently patrol the lines to see that the sentries are alert. The N.C.O. coming on duty will post sentries with the N.C.O. coming off duty. After posting sentries he will report " all correct " or otherwise to the officer on duty.

5. The platoon sergeant will assist the platoon commander generally. He is directly responsible for warning the platoon N.C.Os. for duty by night and day, and will report morning and evening to the platoon commander that he has done so. He will also give their names to the company sergeant-major.

Duties of platoon sergeant.

6. In addition to their other duties section commanders are responsible for personally warning the men of their section for duty by night and day. They will report to the platoon sergeant morning and evening that they have done so.

Duties of section commanders.

N.C.Os. and men will invariably be warned for all duties both verbally and by written rosters posted in the trenches.

A 4

6.—SENTRIES.

By night.

1. The number of sentries required by night will depend on the proximity of the enemy's trench line, the tactical situation, and, above all, the state of our own wire. No fixed rule can be laid down, and brigade commanders will use their discretion in the matter. As a rough guide, for normal conditions, one man in every four should be on sentry from " evening stand-to " until " morning stand-to." If wiring or digging parties are in front this number may be reduced. The reliefs of sentry posts must sleep on the fire-step within touch of the sentry.

2. Sentries will on no account wear waterproof sheets over their heads, nor will their ears be covered in any way by flaps, Balaclava caps, or mufflers.

3. Should a party of the enemy be seen close to our lines the sentry will at once open rapid fire and rouse his relief.

Should the sentry see a working party of the enemy near their own lines he will not fire but will at once send to inform the N.C.O. on duty. The N.C.O. will report to the officer on duty, who will decide whether to open Lewis gun fire.

4. As little challenging as possible will be done by sentries, and then only in a low tone.

By day.

5. The number of sentries required by day will depend largely on whether a good view to the front can be obtained. Normally one to every four bays is sufficient.

Every sentry will be provided with a periscope, except in places where he can safely look over the parapet.

Well-protected look-out posts for sentries will be built along the front trench line.

General rules for sentries.

6. (a) No man will be put on sentry for at least 6 hours after coming off a working party.

(b) Sentries will be posted every 2 hours, except under bad weather conditions, when the length of tour will be reduced.

(c) Every sentry will be regularly posted by an N.C.O., who will explain to him his duties, and ensure that both the sentry and his relief know the position of the section and platoon commanders, the sentries on either side of them, and whether there are any patrols or working parties in front. Should there be salients in our line, the sentry will be carefully instructed so as to avoid any possibility of him firing towards our own trenches.

(d) By night, or in places which have the reputation of being dangerous, i.e., advanced posts, or where the enemy is suspected of mining, sentries should be double.

(e) Sentries will remain standing at all times unless the height of the parapet renders this impossible.

7.—TIME-TABLE.

1. The normal routine of duties will be in accordance with the time-table given below. The actual times will be at the discretion of brigade commanders according to the season of the year :—

One hour before dawn	...	Stand-to.
Before breakfast ...	...	Ration issue.
7.30 a.m.	...	Breakfast.
After breakfast ...	...	Rifle inspection.
9.0 a.m. to 12.30 p.m.	...	Work.
12.30 to 1.30 p.m. ...	...	Dinners.
1.30 to 4.0 p.m. ...	...	Rest.
4.0 to 4.30 p.m. ...	...	Teas.
4.30 to 7.0 p.m. ...	...	Clean-up.
One hour before dark	...	Stand-to.
		Night work.

It is an essential principle that no work should be done at night which can possibly be done by day.

8.—STANDING TO ARMS.

1. Troops will always stand to arms one hour before daylight and one hour before dark. They will remain under arms at morning "Stand to," until the enemy's lines are visible and at evening "Stand to" until darkness sets in.

2. During "stand-to" platoon commanders will inspect the arms, ammunition, and equipment of their men, and satisfy themselves that every man is wearing a box respirator and a P.H. helmet. Ammunition will be made up to 120 rounds per man.

9.—DISCIPLINE.

1. Men must be properly dressed at all times, and as smart and clean as circumstances will allow. **Dress.**

2. All men must shave daily, before the hour for the daily inspection of rifles. **Shaving.**

3. Discipline as regards saluting, standing to attention, &c., will receive as much attention in the trenches as in billets. **Saluting.**

4. No man will leave the trenches without permission from an officer. **Miscellaneous.**

5. All parties moving within the trench area will be correctly marched by an officer or N.C.O.

6. There must be as little talking as possible at night in the front line trenches, as the enemy is in the habit of sending out listening patrols with the object of overhearing our conversation. This is especially important during a relief.

A 5

10.—RIFLES, AMMUNITION AND EQUIPMENT.

Loading of rifles.
1. All rifles in the trenches will have the magazine charged, safety catch to the rear, no cartridge in the chamber. This applies equally to the rifles of sentries.

Care of rifles.
2. Rifle racks (with a small pent-house roof) will be constructed for each bay in front and support trenches. The rifles of all men belonging to that bay (except the sentry) will be kept in the rack during the day. Breach covers will be kept on the rifles.

Where rifle racks do not exist rifles must be placed against the side of the traverse.

By night men will sleep with their rifles by their sides, and their arms through the slings.

In very cold weather sentries will occasionally work the bolt of the rifle, to prevent the striker becoming frozen.

3. Rifles will be thoroughly examined after breakfast daily, and the bolt action will be inspected at morning and evening " stand-to."

Bayonets.
4. In all front line trenches bayonets will invariably be fixed. except on rifles being used for sniping by day.

S.A. Ammunition.
5. Every man will have 120 rounds S.A.A. in his possession. Platoon commanders will have ammunition made up to this amount at morning and evening " stand-to." Ammunition must be kept scrupulously clean. All loading will be from pouch or bandolier, and no ammunition must ever be placed on ground or parapet.

6. All S.A.A. boxes in front and support trenches must be kept in well protected and dry places.

Reserve boxes of S.A.A. will only be opened in case of attack. Boxes will be inspected by platoon commanders at morning " stand-to," to see that the lids work freely, and that the inside lining of the boxes has not been tampered with, and is gas-tight. Any box that has been tampered with will be used for completing pouch ammunition, and will then be returned to battalion headquarters, where it will be replaced. Normally a new box will not be opened until opened boxes are empty.

7. The stock of S.A.A. to be kept in the trenches will be :—
   In front line trenches, 1 box per section.
   At each platoon headquarters, 2 boxes.
   At each company headquarters, 4 boxes.
   At each battalion headquarters, 10 boxes.
   At each brigade headquarters, 50 boxes.

Wearing of equipment.
8. Equipment will always be worn by men in front and support trenches. Belts may be unbuckled. Men in reserve trenches, when off duty, may be permitted to remove their equipment, which must, however, always be close beside them.

Runners, ration and carrying parties, and working parties found from troops out of the line, will carry rifles and one bandolier.

9. Working parties may be permitted to pile or ground arms. Wiring parties in front of the fire trench will sling the rifle.

10. The box respirator will always, without exception, be worn, outside all equipment.

11. Steel helmets will be worn by all ranks in the trench area when outside dugouts.

12. Wounded and men going sick will, if able to walk, wear their equipment and carry their rifles.

Stretcher bearers are responsible that the rifles and equipment of men unable to carry them are taken with them to the dressing station, the ammunition having first been removed from pouches and magazine. Field glasses, wire cutters, &c., will be sent to battalion headquarters.

All rifles and equipment (however badly damaged) of dead men will be collected at battalion headquarters, and handed over to the brigade ammunition dump for return to the base.   Disposal of rifles, ammunition and equipment.

Damaged cartridges and empty cases will be collected and returned to the quartermaster.

13. Officers in the trenches will always be armed.   Officers.

11.—STATE OF READINESS IN FRONT TRENCHES.

1. Every man will be told off to a particular post in case of attack, and, except under orders, or with the permission of his immediate commander, will remain by day and night in such proximity to his post that he can occupy it with the least possible delay. Men must be trained to man the parapet rapidly, both by day and night, on the alarm being given. This can only be done by practice.   Manning the parapet.

2. Officers in a trench should be divided up along its length, and must not be together, especially at night.   Officers.

12.—FIRING BY DAY AND NIGHT.

1. Men will only fire when a target offers itself. If the enemy is in the habit of showing himself at any particular point the attention of the platoon commander should be drawn to it. The latter will inform the battalion sniping officer who will tell off a sniper's post to watch the spot.   Day.

2. A certain number of fixed rifles will be placed in every trench and fired by the sentries. These rifles will be laid on certain selected spots.   Fixed rifles.

3. Indiscriminate firing by day or night is forbidden.   Indiscriminate fire.

In case of attack.

4. If the enemy attacks, rapid fire will be opened without waiting for orders. All fire will be over the parapet and not through loopholes.

13.—ARTILLERY SUPPORT.

Liaison.

1. An artillery liaison officer will be quartered at each battalion headquarters. This officer will visit company commanders in the line during daylight, and will keep the artillery informed about the infantry situation. He will investigate on the spot any cases of short shooting.

Retaliation.

2. Requests for retaliation should be made to this officer, and brigade headquarters should be warned of the action taken.

3. Fire from heavy batteries can, except in the case of the " S.O.S." signal, only be obtained through brigade headquarters. If retaliatory fire is required from heavy batteries it must be stated on what point it is wished that the fire should be directed, or the nature of the hostile fire must be described and the direction from which it came given.

Hostile trench mortars.

4. Any trench mortaring by the enemy should be immediately replied to by Stokes mortars or artillery.

14.—" S.O.S." AND " TEST " SIGNALS.

Occasions on which " S.O.S." signal will be used.

1. In the event of an infantry attack by the enemy, or of a hostile mine being fired the " S.O.S." rockets will be fired and the " S.O.S." signal will at once be sent, the letters S.O.S. being followed by the number of the trench, e.g., " S.O.S., B. 4." (See Sec. **28**, 10.)

All officers will carry this message ready written in their pockets at all times, and on the emergency arising will hand it in to the nearest signal office, whence it will at once be repeated automatically, as a priority message, to every office in the division. The original message need not be signed.

2. On receipt of the S.O.S. signal all batteries covering the trenches concerned will open a concentrated fire on the enemy's front line.

Cancel " S.O.S."

3. When necessity for fire no longer exists the code message for " Cancel S.O.S." and number of trench, will be handed in and dealt with by signals in the same manner as the original " S.O.S." message.

Tests.

4. In order to test the efficient working of the artillery lines, " Test " S.O.S. messages will frequently be sent by signal from the trenches to the supporting battery.

The number of the trench will always be sent, e.g., " Test, A. 6." Rockets will on no account be used for " Test " messages.

The test will consist of one round of shrapnel fired by the battery.

The time taken from the handing in of the message until the shell bursts will be carefully noted by the officer handing in the message and reported to brigade headquarters.

15.—THE BATTALION BOMBING OFFICER.

1. The battalion bombing officer is responsible :—
   (a) That the grenades in his battalion sector are ready detonated, clean, and fit for use.
   (b) That they are properly stored in bomb-proof stores.

16.—CARE OF GRENADES.

1. Only a small percentage of grenades will be kept in the front trenches. These will be kept in a well-protected and dry place.

2. Grenade stores will be built in the end of communication trenches in the support line.

3. Detonators and fuses, except in the front system, will normally be kept in tins, and not in the grenades.

4. The battalion bombing officer will make frequent inspections of all grenades.

17.—MACHINE GUNS.

1. The general scheme of machine gun defence for the divisional sector will be decided by the divisional commander. Machine guns will be echeloned in depth so that in the event of the enemy attacking and gaining a footing in our trenches he may be brought under enfilade fire at every step of his advance.

2. With the exception of a few Vickers guns to be used as anti-raid guns, the defence of the front line will usually be entrusted to Lewis guns.

3. A proportion of machine guns will always be kept in reserve and alloted to the defence of our positions in rear of the front system. Emplacements will be made for these reserve guns and a definite task allotted to them in the scheme of defence.

4. Anti-raid guns will be placed in position by the machine gun company commander in consultation with the divisional machine-gun officer, in accordance with the wishes of the brigadier concerned.

5. With the exception of anti-raid guns and of guns specially posted in rear positions selected by the Corps, the position of all machine guns in the division will be selected by the divisional machine-gun officer, assisted by the machine-gun company commander concerned, in accordance with the divisional scheme. Due regard will be paid to the brigade scheme of defence. These positions will be referred to the brigadier for his approval and subsequently

to the divisional commander. Once the positions have been approved, they will not be changed without reference to divisional headquarters.

6. The divisional machine gun officer will arrange for co-operation between the machine guns of the division and those of the divisions on either flank.

7. Machine gun company commanders are responsible :—

For the condition and upkeep of their guns.

For the construction and upkeep of all emplacements, reserve, alternative or otherwise, by the labour of their machine gun teams.

For the general trench routine being observed by all machine gun teams, as well as any special routine laid down for them.

For the provision of range cards and firing orders in all emplacements.

8. Machine gun company commanders will invariably be warned when artillery are to carry out a bombardment, so that they may be prepared to take advantage of any targets which result.

9. The concealment and protection of machine gun emplacements is important. For this reason, except in case of emergency, machine guns will not be fired from their regular emplacements.

10. Unless emplacements are well concealed, guns will not be mounted, except between evening and morning " stand to."

11. In the front system one man per team will always be on duty with the gun by day and two men by night.

12. Before dusk, while there is still sufficient light, each gun will be laid on its night line.

13. Eight belt boxes and 5,000 rounds of S.A.A. will be maintained in all positions forward of Support Line, and 12 belt boxes and 10,000 rounds S.A.A. in all other positions.

18.—LEWIS GUNS.

1. The number of Lewis guns required for the protection of the front line and their positions will be decided by battalion commanders concerned, assisted by the machine gun company commander. These positions will be inspected by the brigadier, and once his approval has been given will not be altered without reference to brigade headquarters. Guns allotted to these positions will not be used for other purposes.

2. At least one Lewis gun on each battalion front should always be available for accompanying patrols or opening sudden bursts of fire on an enemy working party.

19.—RECONNAISSANCE AND PATROLLING.

1. No Man's Land must be ours. No enemy patrol must be allowed in it.

2. Every battalion in front line must keep the enemy's front trenches under constant observation by night by a system of active patrols.

3. It will be the duty of these patrols to prevent the enemy patrolling and to learn all that there is to be learned about the enemy's front line, the state of his wire, &c. In this way not only will early intimation be given of any hostile attack, *i.e.*, if the enemy is suddenly found to have cut gaps in his wire, but we shall always be aware of the most advantageous spot for carrying out a raid. At the same time the enemy will be prevented from obtaining information about our lines.

4. The battalion front will, for the purpose of patrolling, be divided into sectors. Not more than two patrols should be out on a battalion front at one time. The patrolling carried out by adjacent battalions must be co-ordinated by the battalion commanders.

5. A large scale map of No Man's Land will invariably be kept up at battalion headquarters, on which the observations of patrols will be entered daily. This will ensure all parts of No Man's Land being patrolled. A copy of this map will be handed over on relief.

6. The strength of reconnoitring patrols should normally be one officer or good N.C.O., one bomber, and two rifle men.

7. Patrols will always receive definite orders as to what is required of them before being sent out. They will go out via one listening post (if such exist) and return by another. Each listening post will be warned of the strength of the patrol and the probable hour of departure and return.

8. Word will always be passed *quietly* along the line of sentries when patrols are going out ; sentries will also be informed if it is *not* intended to send out patrols during any particular time.

20.—INTELLIGENCE.

1. The importance of gaining all possible information about the enemy, and of communicating it at once to those above them, must be impressed on all officers.

2. The enemy's line must be kept under continual and minute observation, so that all possible information may be gained about his habits, his movements, his trenches, and his wire. It is particularly essential to locate his machine gun and trench mortar emplacements.

3. This observation will be carried out partly by snipers, but principally by a careful system of observation posts manned by trained observers. The work of the observers will be supervised and co-ordinated by the brigade intelligence officer.

4. As a general rule battalion intelligence officers will arrange for such observation posts as are necessary for watching the enemy's front line system, while the enemy's rear lines will be watched from brigade observation posts.

Daily intelligence report.

5. Battalion intelligence officers will prepare for their battalion commanders a daily report to be submitted to brigade headquarters. This report will describe any new work done by the enemy, and show his activity during the last 24 hours. Anything of especial importance will be forwarded as soon as possible by special report.

Identifications.

6. Information regarding the enemy's units on our front is always of special importance. The only reliable information of this sort is that obtained by contact.

7. The following are the best methods of identifying German units :—

    (a) The marks on identity discs.
    (b) The pay-book (Soldbuch), which has a brown paper cover.
    (c) Letters, diaries, and papers.
    (d) The shoulder strap. It should be stated whether it was taken from a greatcoat or tunic.
    (e) Markings on arms, clothing, and equipment. The number of the regiment is marked on the inside of the flap of the cartridge pouch and on the bayonet near the hilt. It is also stencilled on the tunic lining and inside the cap.

The German soldier usually carries all his papers in the skirt pocket at the back of his tunic. Prisoners will be searched as soon as possible after capture to prevent them destroying documents in their possession.

8. All articles taken from prisoners will be carefully collected and sent in *at once* to divisional headquarters with a statement as to date and place obtained, and whether from prisoners or dead (an estimate of date of death should be given when possible). Captured guns, arms, ammunition, and other stores must be forwarded at once to brigade headquarters and thence to divisional headquarters.

Information re hostile artillery.

9. Great assistance can be given to our artillery by correctly reporting the activity of the hostile guns. The following rules should always be observed when reporting on hostile artillery fire:—

    (i) The time at which the shelling began, and when it ceased.
    (ii) Your own position.
    (iii) Whether howitzer or gun.
    (iv) Direction from which shells arrive. Bearing (true) if possible.
    (v) Whether shells burst in the air or on graze.

(vi) The fuzes of exploded German shells should be sent at once to the nearest artillery unit with a statement as to where they were found.

10. When pointing out the target for our own artillery to engage, its location should always be given by map reference. Datum points should be fixed in the enemy's lines in consultation with the artillery.

11. When reporting results of our own fire the following information must be given :— *Reporting results of our own fire.*

    (i) Your own position.

    (ii) Estimate distances short, over, right, or left, in yards. Avoid vague statements.

    (iii) If shrapnel burst in the air judge whether range is correct by the splash of the bullets on the ground and not by the burst.

21.—DAILY REPORTS.

1. In addition to the intelligence report referred to in Sec. **20**, para. 5, battalions in the line will submit daily reports on the work done in their sub-section for the preceding 24 hours, and brigades will render a daily work report—based on these—to the division on the usual form (*see* Appendix II).

22.—CARE OF HEALTH.

1. Platoon commanders will ensure that every man removes his boots at least once a day for a quarter of an hour, hand-rubs his feet, and turns his socks. In the winter and in wet weather the feet will always be greased once a day, and, if possible dry socks put on.

2. Every scratch from barbed wire, and all small cuts, will be treated at once with iodine. However trivial the wound it must be dressed by the medical officer as soon as possible.

3. A drying room should, whenever possible, be improvised in every company by means of braziers in dug-outs. Men's clothing, especially socks, should be dried at the first opportunity.

4. Instructions on care of feet are given in Appendix III.

23.—SANITATION.

1. Special precautions must be taken to keep trenches in a clean and sanitary state. *Trenches.*

2. Latrines will be dug in convenient places. In dry weather the best system is to dig a hole 6 feet to 8 feet deep, covered over either with box seats or with boards placed close together. With the latter system one board is removed when the latrine is used, and should be replaced at once after use. This system obviates all smell, and does away with the necessity for detailing fatigue parties *Latrines.*

to empty latrine buckets, but in wet weather the deep hole is liable to collapse and a removal system utilising buckets, biscuit tins, &c., must be substituted for it.

Urine buckets.

3. Urine buckets will be placed beside the latrine, and will be emptied by the sanitary squad.

Chlorate of lime.

4. A supply of chloride of lime or creosote will be kept in each trench and will be freely used.

Filling in latrines.

5. Full or disused latrines will be filled in and a notice " old latrine " put over them.

Sanitary squad.

6. Battalion commanders will hold the sanitary squad responsible under the battalion medical officer for the cleanliness of latrines.

Refuse pits.

7. Refuse pits must be dug, and all remains of food, tea leaves, &c., thrown into them. When a pit is full, it should be covered with earth, and a notice put over it " foul ground."

Duties of medical officers.

8. The medical officer attached to battalions must visit the trenches constantly and bring to the notice of company and platoon commanders any points which require improvement, paying particular attention to latrines, water supply, and refuse pits. His orders on these points will be considered as coming from the battalion commander.

The A.D.M.S. will inspect the trenches in company with the battalion medical officers and officer commanding affiliated Field Ambulance at least once a month, and will report to divisional headquarters the result of this inspection, together with any suggestions for the improvement of sanitation. He will forward a copy of his report to the brigade concerned.

Burials.

9. Bodies of dead men will be buried in one of the burial grounds detailed in brigade orders. If this cannot be done, care must be taken to select a site where they will not be likely to interfere with future work on support trenches, &c.

24.—COOKING.

1. Cooking must be done under section, platoon, or company arrangements, according to which is most convenient, and must be carried out at regular hours.

2. Individual cooking in the trenches is forbidden, except in very exceptional circumstances. Permission must be obtained from the brigade commander, who should grant it sparingly.

3. As little smoke as possible must be made by the cook's fires.

4. Unused rations will be returned to the quartermaster.

5. Arrangements should be made that soup or some hot drink is available for the men between midnight and 4 a.m.

25.—RATION PARTIES.

1. Ration parties will as a rule be found from the supports and reserves.

2. If this is not possible, and it is necessary that men from the front trenches have to be employed, not more than 10 per cent. of the men in the firing line are to be away from the trenches at the same time.

3. Ration parties from the supports and reserves will, so far as possible, consist of complete units.

4. Ration and all other carrying parties must make as little noise as possible.

26.—RUM ISSUE.

1. If rum is issued in the trenches, the following rules will be observed :—

 (i) Rum will never be issued to the men on an empty stomach.

 (ii) The supply will be kept by the company commander or trench commander (officer).

 (iii) Rum will only be issued in the presence of an officer, who will see that it is consumed only by the man to whom it has been issued.

 (iv) Any surplus of an issue of rum may be kept by the company commander or the officer i/c a trench for issue on special occasions at the discretion of the commanding officer.

27.—SALVAGE.

1. All rifles, ammunition (including fired cases), equipment, tools, trench stores, &c., found lying about must invariably be collected and returned to battalion headquarters, whence they will be forwarded to the Brigade salvage dump.

2. At intervals throughout the trenches sandbags or specially made boxes will be hung up as receptacles for loose or dirty S.A.A., empty cases, and chargers. Others will be hung up for waste paper and rubbish, and the receptacles will be labelled accordingly. These bags or boxes will be cleared daily under battalion arrangements.

3. Nothing should ever be left lying about in the trenches, which must be kept scrupulously clean. The fire step must always be kept clear. Untidy trenches invariably denote lack of discipline in the unit concerned.

28.—SPECIAL INSTRUCTIONS.

1. Every officer and man must know :—

 The names of all posts and trenches in his vicinity.

 The names of all marked features behind the enemy's line.

 The position of his company and battalion headquarters, and the shortest way to them.

 The position of the support line and reserve line.

 The position of the first-aid post.

2. Officers in the trenches will not carry on them any papers, orders, or documents which would give information of value to the enemy if captured.

3. Maps or sketches showing our dispositions, defences, &c., must on no account be taken beyond battalion headquarters.

4. No man will ever leave his firing position to attend to wounded. No men other than stretcher bearers will accompany wounded to the first-aid post or to the rear.

5. The word " Retire " is never to be used.

6. The enemy must never know what it is to have a quiet day, but must continually be kept with his nerves on stretch. Every man in the trenches must try to do something each day to cause loss to the enemy and to improve and strengthen our position.

Hostile aircraft. 7. On the approach of any of the enemy's aircraft three blasts will be blown on a whistle. This is the signal for all ranks to keep perfectly still.

Two blasts on the whistle will indicate that the aircraft has moved away.

Enemy aircraft will not be fired on without the order of an officer or N.C.O. who will satisfy himself that the aircraft is hostile.

If a Zeppelin is sighted a priority message will be sent notifying where the Zeppelin was seen, the direction in which it was moving, and the time at which it was observed and by whom. If map squares are referred to the number of the sheet should be given.

Neither aeroplanes nor airships will be fired upon by night, unless they unmistakably reveal that they are hostile by dropping bombs, by opening fire, or by being clearly recognisable as hostile in the light of a searchlight.

Action in the event of being taken prisoner. 8. All ranks will be warned that, should they find themselves in the hands of the enemy, it is only necessary for them to give their true number and name. No other information whatever will be given.

Assistance to R.E. 9. All possible assistance when asked for must be given to R.E. and miners working in the section held by a brigade.

Sign posts. 10. Sign posts will always be placed at all trench junctions, and at frequent intervals in all communication avenues.

Notice boards. Trenches will be divided into sections, each with a name, e.g., F. 1, F. 2, F. 3, &c., the numbers running from right to left. A notice board will be placed at each end of each section, giving the name of the section. Thus, on the right of F. 2, there will be two boards, as follows : " F. 2," " F. 1." Bays will be numbered from right to left in each section, and a small board affixed giving its designation, e.g., " F. 2, Bay 1," " F. 2, Bay 3," &c. Notice boards will also be placed over all stores of ammunition, grenades, &c.

11. A conservancy party of one N.C.O. and six men will be detailed to each main communication trench. They will collect all material dropped by carrying parties, replace broken trench boards, keep all drains open, &c., and generally be responsible for the upkeep of the trench. *Trench wardens*

PART III.—WORK ON TRENCHES.

29.—DIVISION OF RESPONSIBILITY BETWEEN DIVISION AND BRIGADES.

1. On taking over a portion of the line divisional headquarters will lay down which trenches are to be kept up by divisional labour and which by brigade labour. Generally, brigades will be responsible for all work as far back as the reserve line inclusive, the division being responsible for all work in rear of that line.

2. When the division is in the line one field company and one pioneer company will normally be affiliated to each brigade.

30.—IMPROVEMENT OF DEFENCES.

1. Work on the improvement of the defences must be carried on unceasingly. The importance of systematic work must be recognised, and a programme should be drawn up at the beginning of a tour in the trenches.

31.—WIRE PARTIES.

1. The rifle section of each platoon will be specially trained in wiring. Wiring parties from these sections will be employed nightly on improving and extending our wire. Wiring parties should report when they go out and come in, in order that sentries and units on the flanks may be warned.

32.—NOTES ON TRENCH CONSTRUCTION.

1. The following essential requirements must be first attended to in a trench :—

    (a) Parapet must be shell proof.
    (b) Every man must be able to fire over the parapet.
    (c) Traverses must be adequate.
    (d) There must be a good wire entanglement.

2. Loopholes must be made for use by snipers during the day. They should never face straight to the front; they should be blinded, and should have a curtain (sandbag or waterproof sheet) hung on the firing side, to be used in the same way as a photographer's black *Loopholes.*

cloth. It is essential that the enemy should not be allowed to snipe. All ranks should be on the lookout for places, not necessarily in the front line, whence sniping can be carried out with success.

Advantage of daylight work.

3. Work in the trenches should be done in daylight as much as possible. Day work is more efficient and less tiring to the men than night work. Night work must be reconnoitred in daylight, and the work carefully detailed and organized.

Fire and support trenches.

4. Fire and support trenches will normally be 7 feet in height from the top of the floor-board to the top of the parapet. They will be provided with a fire-step running the whole length of each bay, and will be of sufficient width to permit of free passage in rear of it. They must be well revetted, preferably with strutted frames, giving a minimum height of $6\frac{1}{2}$ feet from the top of the floor-board to the strut.

Communication trenches.

5. Communication trenches will be similarly revetted where necessary with strutted frames as above. These trenches will be 7 feet 6 inches in height from the top of the floor-board to the top of the parapet, and about $2\frac{1}{2}$ feet wide at the bottom. Wherever possible they should be constructed for use as fire trenches and wired on both sides, in order to form a defensive pocket should the enemy succeed in penetrating that part of our line.

Drainage.

6. A comprehensive drainage system must be constructed in order to avoid the water from one trench draining into another. In certain soils it will be possible to effect the drainage of the trenches by means of deep sumps constructed at frequent intervals some 6 feet in rear of the trench or under the trench boards. In other cases a complete system of drainage ditches will have to be dug.

Shelters.

7. The practice of undercutting trenches to obtain shelter is strictly forbidden and no shelters will be constructed which in any way interfere with the use of the fire-step, or with free passage along the trench.

33.—WORKING PARTIES.

1. All work on a front trench will be carried out by the garrison of the trench, assisted where necessary by the garrison of the support and reserve trenches. Work in rear of the front trenches will be carried out by the garrisons of the support and reserve trenches.

2. Covering parties will always be provided for digging and wiring parties in front of the front trench.

3. Working or carrying parties from support or reserve battalions, or from a brigade out of the line, working in the defence section of a battalion occupying front line trenches, will, in the event of attack, be at the disposal of the battalion commander in whose section they are working. Similarly, parties from brigades out of the line working in rear of battalion headquarters but in front of brigade headquarters, will, in the event of attack, be at the disposal of the brigade concerned.

4. The officer or N.C.O. in command of a working party of more than 30 men which does not belong to the normal garrison of the section will invariably send an orderly to brigade or battalion head-quarters, as the case may be, to notify the exact position at which he is working, and to ask for orders in case of attack. The form shown below will be used for this purpose. It will be completed by the addition of the necessary instructions, initialled by an officer of the brigade or battalion headquarters and returned by the orderly to the working party concerned.

To   ⎰ ....Infantry Brigade.
Headquarters ⎱ ....Battalion...............Regiment.

Orders in case of attack requested for working party.

............officers..................other ranks.

Working at..

From............................. to...................................

Date........................... Signature........................

It is most important that instructions to ensure the above order being carried out be given to the officer in command of every working party.

5. Working parties will invariably consist of complete units, *i.e.*, a section, platoon, or company. The authority ordering a working party will state the number of men required, and the officer detailing the troops will tell off the necessary companies, platoons, sections, &c., to make a total not less than the number ordered.

6. Definite tasks will be allotted to all working parties, and the party will not be marched off until the task is finished. The com-mander of the party should know what work is expected from it before it commences work, so that no time is wasted in getting to work. Officers and N.C.Os. detailed with working parties must clearly understand that they are present for the specific purpose of assisting in the superintendence of work. Even when working under engineer supervision the commander of a working party is responsible that the work done satisfies all requirements.

7. Working parties found by brigades out of the line will not wear equipment, but will carry rifle and one bandolier.

8. All parties working within range of the enemy's artillery will be provided with a proportion of stretcher bearers, who will be included in the strength of the party, and, until required for duty as stretcher bearers, will carry out a task.

9. When parties are detailed to work at night, or at hours which interfere with their normal meal hours, commanding officers will make such arrangements as are necessary for the party to be supplied

with haversack rations, or for cookers to accompany the party to the rendezvous. In the latter case arrangements will be made for the party to move off early so that the men may have finished their meal before the hour at which the party is detailed to report.

34.—MINES.

Secrecy as to mines.

1. If mine shafts exist, or mining is in progress in a sector of trenches held by the division, it is most important that no mention of the fact should be made, especially in back areas.

Disposal of sand-bags from mines.

2. When mining is in progress on a brigade front, the brigade concerned will supply working parties to remove the bags filled with shail from the mine. The bags will either be used where required for the construction of defences, or their contents will be scattered on dumping grounds selected by the brigadier. On no account are the bags to be allowed to block trenches or dugouts.

Precautions when one of our mines is exploded.

3. In the event of one of our mines being exploded, a clear space of 5 yards will be kept on either side of the mouth of the mine shaft.

4. Should the enemy fire a mine in or near our trenches, the crater formed will immediately be occupied by the nearest troops. This order will be made known to all ranks.

Enemy mine craters.

PART IV.—ACTION IN CASE OF ATTACK.

35.—DEFENCE SCHEMES.

General principles.

1. Commanders of all units will prepare schemes for the defence of their sector, and communicate them to all concerned. The following general principles will be observed :—

(a) The main front line of trenches must be held to the last, whatever happens.

(b) It is the duty of the immediate supports, without waiting for orders, to reinforce the front line of trenches if required, and, if any trench is captured, to counter-attack at once without hesitation. Similarly if a trench is blown up it is their duty to occupy the crater at once.

(c) The battalion reserve will be used to maintain the front line of trenches intact, and to re-capture any trenches lost. Should the attack be on such a large scale that the battalion reserve is insufficient to attempt the re-establishment of the line it will occupy a position to check any further advance until a counter-attack by the brigade reserve can be organized.

36.—COUNTER ATTACKS.

1. As soon as possible after taking over a new line, commanders will submit to their immediate commander their scheme for counter-attacking the enemy as above, should he gain possession of the whole or any part of the line. In framing this scheme it must be remembered that in every line of trenches there are certain points which would be of value to the enemy if captured, whereas there are others which would be of little use to him.

2. All officers and N.C.Os. will thoroughly reconnoitre the trenches on their right and left so as to be able to lead any immediate counter-attack that may be required.

3. Counter-attacks made at once and without hesitation will usually be successful even if made by small numbers ; but a counter-attack, once the enemy has been given time to establish himself, is a very difficult and costly operation.

37.—GAS ATTACKS.

1. The action to be taken in the event of a gas attack is described in Part V.   Gas attacks.

38.—LIQUID FIRE.

1. It should be explained to all ranks that the " Flammenwerfer " is a short range weapon only, and that its effect has proved small when the troops have kept their heads. The best means of defeating a liquid fire attack is to shoot the carriers before they get within their own effective range. Failing this, as it is impossible for the enemy to direct the flame into a trench from a position above it, the troops in front line should lie down on their faces close under the parapet, while the troops in the support line open rapid rifle fire and Lewis gun fire on the point of attack.

2. The " Flammenwerfer " used in co-operation with bombers advancing up a trench must be defeated by other bombers stationed behind traverses.

39.—BRIGADE RESERVE.

1. Unless otherwise ordered, units in brigade reserve must be in an instant state of readiness. When a unit is resting special instructions will usually be issued as to the state of readiness to be observed. If none are issued men may take off their boots and puttees, but alarm posts must always be fixed and arrangements made for turning out speedily in case of necessity. On the alarm being given all units will fall in at once on their alarm posts, and send a mounted officer to brigade headquarters.

2. All units will reconnoitre routes from their rest billets to all sections of the front line held by the division. They will also reconnoitre the ground behind the front line in order that they may

be able to utilise it tactically to the best advantage should the necessity arise.

40.—STRONG POINTS.

1. Officers in charge of strong points for all-round defence are responsible that :—

    (i) The post has sufficient reserve of ammunition, food, and water for 48 hours, and a sufficient number of tools.

    (ii) The post is not abandoned in any circumstances whatsoever, without a direct order from brigade headquarters.

    (iii) The ranges to prominent points are known by all the garrison.

41.—BATTLE POLICE.

1. In the case of attack, battle police posts will be placed in all communication trenches with orders to prevent any man withdrawing from the front line.

2. Battle police will only let men pass who have a distinguishing badge or show a pass.

PART V.—PRECAUTIONS AGAINST GAS.

42.—ROUTINE PRECAUTIONS.

1. Full instructions on this subject are given in S.S. 534. The following paragraphs indicate the more important details that should be known to all ranks.

2. Officers commanding units down to batteries and companies are assisted by a specially-trained gas N.C.O. in taking the necessary precautions against gas (*vide* para. 4).

3. The direction of the wind must always be carefully watched, wind vanes being erected for this purpose near all headquarters down to companies and batteries. Gas alert will be ordered when the wind is in the dangerous quarter, no matter what the strength of the wind. The order " Gas alert " will be sent out to all units by divisional headquarters, but brigade headquarters or battalion commanders are empowered to order a " Gas alert " as a result of wind observations forwarded by company commanders. Such action will be reported immediately to the next higher formation. " Gas alert " notices should be posted at the entrance to each main communication trench and at other suitable points within divisional areas. On taking over a new front divisional headquarters will notify all concerned of the " dangerous quarter " referred to above.

4. In order to avoid casualties from the enemy's gas the following precautions are essential :— **Routine precautions.**

    (a) Strict compliance with the instructions issued (para. 1 above) regarding the carrying, inspection and renewal of box respirators and gas helmets and with the instructions contained in S.S. 534 for the training of all ranks in the use of anti-gas appliances.

    (b) The maintenance of an efficient system of giving an alarm in case of a gas attack. It is essential that the Strombos horns or gas gongs should be situated at intervals sufficiently close to ensure that the alarm is carried back at least as far as brigade headquarters, even when heavy firing is in progress.

    (c) The efficient protection of all dug-outs and ammunition recesses by blankets sprayed with solution.

    (d) The maintenance of gas-clearing apparatus, flapper fans for trenches and shelters, braziers and fuel for deep dug-outs.

5. Box respirators will always be carried in the " Alert " position when within the trench system.

43.—GAS ALERT.

1. When the " Gas Alert " is put into force (*vide* para. 3 above) the following precautions will be taken :— **Gas alert.**

    (a) All the helmets and box respirators will be carefully inspected on the "gas alert" being ordered and will subsequently be inspected daily.

    (b) Company and battery gas N.C.Os. will report to company and battery headquarters at once. They will inspect daily all anti-gas apparatus, Strombos horns, flapper fans, vacuum bulbs, and gas testing tubes, and stores of fuel for clearing dug-outs. They will see that gas-proof dug-outs are in good order, and the blanket curtain sprayed.

    (c) All ranks in the trench system whose small box respirator has for any reason become unserviceable, will carry the P.H. helmet on the chest in the " Alert " position.

    (d) Men wearing P.H. helmets in the " Alert " position will not remove their jackets, neither will they wear mufflers nor mackintosh sheets round their necks. Nothing will be slung across the chest in such a manner as to interfere with the rapid adjustment of the helmet.

    (e) The reserve helmet will be carried in the satchel attached to the belt or slung from the left shoulder *perpendicularly downwards* under the belt. It is particularly important that the reserve helmet should be accessible in cold weather, as the rubber expiratory valve of the small box respirator is very liable to become frozen, and breathing through it merely aggravates the danger owing to the subsequent freezing of the condensed moisture.

(*f*) All working parties will post a sentry to give instant warning of a gas attack. This is particularly important in the case of men working outside our parapet.

(*g*) Men detailed to sound Strombos horns or gongs will take post.

(*h*) A sentry will be posted at every dug-out holding more than 10 men, and also at each group of two or three smaller dug-outs.

(*i*) A sentry will be posted at each headquarters signal office and by each detached party.

(*j*) The duties of all sentries are :—

    (1) To give warning of a gas attack.
    (2) To adjust the blanket curtain of gas-proof dug-outs immediately after giving an alarm.

(*k*) At night sentries will have at least two men within reach of them so that the alarm can be spread rapidly.

(*l*) Troops behind the trench system will sleep with one gas helmet or respirator round their necks, and have the second helmet available.

(*m*) All telephone lines will be tested.

(*n*) Medical officers will check the proportion of ammonia capsules and other first-aid supplies for gas cases which are maintained with stretcher bearers in the front line.

44.—HOSTILE GAS ATTACKS.

1. The earliest warning of a cloud gas attack is given :—

(*a*) By the hissing noise of the gas escaping from the cylinders.

(*b*) By the appearance of a cloud of any colour over the enemy trenches. If the attack takes place at night the cloud will not be visible from a distance.

(*c*) By the smell of the gas in listening posts.

Any man noticing any of the above signs will immediately give the " gas alarm," which will be transmitted by all available means, Strombos horns, gongs, and buzzer. The message " gas," followed by the number of the trench, *e.g.*, " Gas, B. 4," will be kept ready written by every officer and handed in to the nearest signal office. It will then be sent priority to all offices in the division, as in case of " S.O.S." messages (*vide* Sec. **14**, 1).

The following action will also be taken :—

(*a*) Sentries will warn all ranks in the immediate vicinity, and these men will pass the warning on. The special sentries posted over dug-outs (*vide* para. 5 (*h*) above) will themselves turn out all the men in them.

(b) All ranks will put on respirators directly the alarm is sounded. .

(c) Troops will man their parapets quietly.

(d) *All unnecessary movement will cease.* Supporting or relieving troops will not be moved unless the tactical situation requires it.

(e) Blankets on protected dug-outs will be lowered, and carefully adjusted.

(f) Men will not remain in dug-outs unless their duty requires them to.

(g) Box respirators must be worn in all dug-outs whether protected or unprotected.

(h) Infantry in front trenches will get ready to fire. They will on no account open a heavy fire until an infantry attack develops, but occasional short bursts should be fired from Lewis and machine guns, and occasional shots from rifles, to prevent an accumulation of fouling.

All batteries will be turned on to the hostile trenches from which the gas is issuing, and also on the enemy's support lines, as it is the practice of the infantry to retire to these lines when gas is being discharged. A light barrage should also be put up in front of the enemy's lines to prevent hostile patrols from following up the gas.

Troops in the front line not affected by gas must be prepared to bring a cross fire to bear on the enemy attempting to advance against a gassed portion of the trench.

(i) Should an infantry attack develop, but not before, the normal " S.O.S." procedure will be carried out.

(k) During the gas attack all men will be continually on the look-out to help one another in the event of the respirators being damaged by fire or accidents. Wounded men have a tendency to try and remove their respirators. They will be watched and prevented from doing this.

(l) Ammunition which the gas is passing will be protected by placing it under blankets soaked with anti-gas solution, or by placing it in protected dug-outs. Machine guns, Lewis guns, and L.T.M.'s not actually in action will be protected by waterproof sheets on top of which anti-gas blankets are placed.

(m) Pigeons will be protected by placing flannel bags soaked with solution over the baskets. These bags are provided by the signal service.

At the end of a gas attack the " gas " message will be cancelled by sending " Cancel gas " and the number of the trench, as in the case of " Cancel S.O.S." (*vide* Sec. 14).

2. In the event of the enemy projecting gas cylinders and drums and the resulting cloud showing signs of being carried for a long distance, the same action will be taken as for a cloud gas attack.

45.—GAS SHELLS.

1. Every precaution must be taken to guard against the effects of a bombardment with gas shells and trench mortar bombs. Such a bombardment is liable to be overlooked until it is too late owing to the lethal gas shells being mixed with those that are lachrymatory or with ordinary high explosive shells. Gas shells may be distinguished by their small detonation, often giving the impression that they are blinds, by the formation of a whitish cloud over the ground shelled, and by their lachrymatory or asphyxiating effect. In the event of a bombardment by shells and bombs giving small detonations :—

(a) Box respirators will be immediately put on in the area shelled and kept on until ordered to take them off by an officer.

(b) All dug-outs and shelters in the vicinity will be visited and sleeping men roused. Blankets on dug-outs will be lowered.

(c) Horns will *not* be sounded, but gongs and rattles will be used and the alarm passed round from man to man.

(d) All instances of shelling by gas shells will be reported to divisional headquarters for investigation by the divisional gas officer.

(e) The same precautions as to clearing trenches and dug-outs will be taken as after a cloud gas attack (**see** next section).

46.—PROCEDURE AFTER A GAS ATTACK.

1. After a gas attack, box respirators will not be removed until permission has been given by the company or battery commander. When permission has been given to take off respirators all ranks will at once readjust them in the " alert " position, so as to be ready for a subsequent gas cloud. The enemy constantly adopts the plan of stopping a discharge of gas for 10 or 20 minutes in order to catch men who have taken off their respirators in the belief that the attack is over. Dug-outs will not be entered without respirators until they have been cleared of all traces of gas by flappers and fires ; they will not be re-occupied for three hours after being cleared. Troops who have undergone a gas attack will be relieved of all movements and fatigues for the subsequent 24 hours. Rifles and machine guns must

be immediately cleaned with oil and subsequently with boiling water and soda as soon as possible.

A sharp look-out will be maintained as long as the wind continues in a dangerous quarter, and men will sleep on the fire step within reach of a sentry. A subsequent gas cloud is always likely.

PART VI.—COMMUNICATIONS.

47.—GENERAL INSTRUCTIONS.

1. It is the duty of all ranks to assist signals in the following ways :—

(a) Reporting breaks in lines to nearest signal station.

(b) Taking care to prevent damage to lines by troops or wagons, even if lines are badly laid.

(c) Bringing into brigade headquarters any telephone equipment, spare drums, &c., found lying about.

(d) Preventing any unauthorised person interfering with lines ; any one seen interfering with cables who has not a blue and white armlet should be asked his business, and sent to brigade headquarters if answers are not satisfactory ; any civilians touching lines should immediately be arrested.

2. The signalling officer is responsible for the communications of his battalion. Battalion signals are responsible for all communications from battalion headquarters forward.

3. All disused or unlabelled wires will be reeled up.

4. All wires must be pinned into the sides of trenches, infantry wires on the south and east sides, artillery wires on the north and west sides ; and all wires must be properly labelled.

5. Where roads, tracks, or communication trenches are crossed by telephone lines, the wires must be buried, or put up at such a height as not to impede movement. If it is found necessary to lay temporary lines, e.g., as in the case of a F.O.O., these must be laid on the top of the sides of communication trenches and on the top of the parados of fire trenches.

6. It must be realised that in the event of heavy shelling all telephonic communication is likely to be interrupted, and an efficient alternative system of visual signalling or service of orderlies must be arranged and tested.

48.—SPECIAL PRECAUTIONS AGAINST HOSTILE LISTENING APPARATUS.

1. The enemy has brought his listening apparatus to such a state of perfection that all instruments within 3,000 yards of the front line are in the danger zone. Any instruments further in rear, when

in direct communication with an instrument in the danger zone, must be considered as coming for the time being within the danger zone, so far as precautions to be taken are concerned.

2. To prevent the enemy obtaining valuable information by means of his listening apparatus the following instructions will be strictly adhered to :—

(a) All circuits must be truly metallic, the line and return being laid in the closest proximity.

(b) Every signal office will be allotted a position call. This call will not be changed when one unit relieves another. Units and formations will be allotted code names, and trench code books will be issued under army arrangements.

(c) The telephone (conversation or buzzer) will be used for official communication only, all private conversation being absolutely forbidden. Position calls and not code names will be used for calling up and testing the line, and for stating the position of the speaker. Code names will be used only in the body of the conversation and as little as possible. The trench code book will be used for all operation messages, except as stated in para. (f) below, but conversations dealing with official matters, which are of no value to the enemy, may be carried on in clear. In all messages units will be referred to by code names, and not in clear.

(d) When writing messages to be sent by buzzer, code names will be written both in the address and in the body of the message, but before the message is transmitted the transmitsing office will convert the code names in the addresses to and from into the position calls of the signal office concerned. This will apply equally if the message is eventually sent over the lines by speech. All messages will be signed by an officer, who will be held personally responsible for the contents of the message sent, and for seeing that it is sent in code if necessary.

(e) Pigeons, visual, or wireless, all of which are liable to interception, will be used for important messages only when the employment of runners is impracticable. All wireless messages will be sent in B.A.B. code or cipher. They will either be enciphered before handing in to signals or will be marked " to be enciphered by W.T. operator," and signed by the officer sending the message.

(f) In cases of great emergency senior officers (brigade and battalion commanders) will exercise their discretion in using the telephone or the buzzer as a medium for conveying operation orders or other important messages in clear. Officers taking advantage of this permission will be held responsible for their action, and must be prepared to justify it.

3. Any officer, except as in (*f*) above, N.C.O., or man who, within the danger zone, refers by telephone or buzzer to matters which if overheard by the enemy would be to the latter's advantage will be tried by Field General Court Martial.

4. The term "buzzer," wherever it occurs in this section includes power buzzers.

5. Where Fullerphones are installed, they may be used for sending *by key* any message in clear. They are no protection in the case of spoken messages.

C. F. ASPINALL,

Lieut.-Colonel G.S.,

63rd (R.N.) Division.

17th August, 1917.

Appendix I.

LIST OF TRENCH STORES.

The following are trench stores and will be handed and taken over with the trenches :—

Bombs.
Bomb throwers.
Gum boots (thigh).
Braziers.
Barrels, water.
Buckets, earth (or pails, earth).
Buckets, latrine.
Brooms.
Catapults.
Compasses, prismatic.
Costumes, snipers and camouflage.
Costumes, acid proof.
Flapper fans.
Grenades.
Gongs, bells and apparatus for warning gas attacks.
Loopholed plates.
Ladders.
Lights, " Very " (those stored in trenches only).
Megaphones.
Periscopes, No. 9.
Receptacles for water.
Rods, measuring.
Rammers.
Rifle rests.
Rockets and stands.
Rifle batteries (the rifles are regimental equipment).
S.A.A. reserves (any reserves kept in the trenches and not on the man).
Stands, rifle grenade.
Syringes.
Soyers stoves.
Stretchers, trench.
Scoops, water.
Sticks, microphone.
Tapes, measuring.
Tapes, tracing.
Telephone wire (*in situ*).
Telescopes, observation post.
Trench mortars (not in batteries nor on R.A. charge).
Weather cocks.
Washing basins.
Wire, barbed and plain.

Wheel barrows and hand barrows

Vermorel sprayers and solution.

Veils, observers'.

R.E. trench stores—entrenching tools and all items from R.E. Parks (except those held on charge of units under Mob. Store Tables), such as axes felling, bill-hooks, crowbars, chisels, hammers, mauls, picks, pumps and mining tools, reaping hooks, and sickles, saws, shovels and spades, boring tools, hoes, mud scrapers and scrapers.

Primus stoves.

Food containers.

Flash spotters.

Klaxon horns.

Strombus horns.

Machine-gun mountings, pivoting.

Machine-gun carriers.

Overalls, night scouts'.

Observation plates.

Steel shelters.

Knob kerries.

Thermos cases.

Rifle rest, rowlock.

*Anemometers.

Boots, lumberman's, and stockings.

Disinfectors, thresh.

*Fire extincteurs.

*Lanterns, tent, or lamps, hurricane, used in huts or tents

*Lamps used in huts.

*Latrine buckets.

*Periscopes above establishment of units, and all loophole periscopes.

*Petrol cans for carriage of water to trenches.

*Rifle sniperscopes above establishment.

*Rifles, telescopic, above establishment.

*Rifles, large bore.

*Shields for bombers.

Soyers stoves (those in trenches are trench stores).

*Tents and tent bottoms.

*Trench cookers.

*Stoves for heating officers' billets, huts, and dug-outs.

Vacuum bulbs.

Washing tubs and basins (those in trenches are trench stores).

NOTE.—The stores marked * should be left in the divisional areas when a relief takes over, and will be included in the list of stores handed over.

Those of the above stores which are in the trenches are to be regarded as trench stores.

Appendix II.

DAILY REPORT BY G.O.C. INFANTRY BRIGADE IN THE LINE.

63RD DIVISION.

Daily report by G.O.C.................................Infantry Brigade.

For 24 hours ending..1916.

1. Work done on trenches (not to include draining, baling, or strengthening of parapets).*	
2. Work done on communication trenches.	
3. Work done on 2nd Line system.	
4. Any special working parties not included in (1), (2) and (3).	
5. Any suggestions or requirements	
6. Results of any artillery tests carried out.	

Signature ....

Commanding...

* Actual distances dug to be given, together with depth and width. In case of parapets, state length revised or repaired, or extent to which height has been raised. Nature of repairs to be stated.

NOTES.—Work of a routine nature, such as baling, &c., is not required under para. 1 ; it is taken for granted that this is carried out.

This report is to accompany the Intelligence Report.

Appendix III.

PREVENTION OF CHILLED FEET AND FROSTBITE.

1. Chilled feet and frostbite are caused by :—
   (a) Prolonged standing in cold water or mud.
   (b) The continued wearing of wet socks, boots, and puttees.
   (c) The blood circulation in the feet and legs being interfered with by the use of tight boots, tight puttees, or other pressure on the lower limbs.

2. They can be prevented or diminished by :—
   (a) Improvements to trenches, i.e., foot-boards, drainage, and pumps.
   (b) By reducing the time spent in the trenches as far as the military situation permits.
   (c) By ensuring that, so far as is possible, men enter the trenches warmly clad in dry boots, socks, trousers, and puttees, and with the skin well rubbed with whale oil, mineral jelly, or anti-frostbite grease.
   (d) By movement, when possible, so as to maintain blood circulation.
   (e) By the provision of warmth, shelter, hot food, and facilities for washing the feet and drying the wet clothes of men leaving the trenches.

3. In order to minimise the prevalence of chilled feet and frost-bite, commanding officers will be held responsible that the following instructions are carried out under the strictest supervision :—
   (a) Before entering the trenches, feet and legs will be washed and dried, then well rubbed with whale oil or anti-frostbite grease and dry socks put on.   It is of the utmost importance that whale oil or anti-frostbite grease should not merely be applied, but *thoroughly rubbed in until the skin is dry.*   Unless this is done the oil and grease are to a great measure valueless, for it is the hand-rubbing more than the oil which does good.
   b) A second pair of dry socks (two pairs if possible) will be carried by each man and, where possible, arrangements will be made for socks to be dried and re-issued, so that each man gets a clean dry pair every 24 hours.
   (c) While in the trenches, boots, socks and puttees are to be taken off by every man at least once in 24 hours, the feet rubbed for 20 minutes and dried, and a dry pair of socks put on, if available, after greasing the feet.
   (d) On no account will hot water be used, nor the feet held near a fire.
   (e) Hot food must be provided during tours of duty in the trenches.

   Hot soup, tea or cocoa should be issued in the early

morning or late evening, or both—preferably between the hours of 1 to 4 a.m., when vitality is at its lowest.

(f) Where circumstances admit, long gum boots will be put on while the men's feet are dry, before entering wet trenches, in order that men may start their tour of duty with dry feet.

4. Gum boots, thigh, are issued to units according to the nature of the trenches held. These boots are solely issued for men actually in the trenches.

If a man is remaining stationary for some time in a dry place, *e.g.*, a sentry, it is advisable to take off the gum boots and put on boots and puttees, as the socks become damp through perspiration if gum boots are worn for any length of time.

5. Arrangements must be made for drying gum boots. This is best done by allotting a dug-out with a brazier as a gum boot store, with a man in charge, whose duty it will be to hang the gum boots up, foot upwards. This is the simplest method of handing over gum boots in the front line in a dry condition to a relieving unit.

6. The following points will also be found useful :—

(a) Leather boots should be kept well greased and dubbined, and the laces should be sound and without knots.

(b) Boots should be at least a size too large. When boots are large enough, it is well to wear two pairs of socks ; but this is dangerous if the boots are small, as it leads to further pressure on the feet. Puttees should never be worn tightly.

(c) The general circulation can be kept up by keeping the body warm and dry. A mackintosh sheet worn over the greatcoat in the trenches is of assistance when no waterproof is available. Care should, however, be taken to prevent men arriving in the trenches in a state of perspiration, as this is a frequent cause of chill. It is therefore undesirable to wear mackintosh sheets over the greatcoats on the way up. It is better to carry the greatcoat rolled, on the march, and wear the mackintosh cape or waterproof sheet alone over the equipment. The greatcoat will thus be dry to put on on arrival.

(d) The stretcher bearers and R.A.M.C. personnel of the unit should undergo a course of " massage " at a Field Ambulance, after which they themselves should instruct as many men of their units as possible.

(e) On return to billets after a tour in the trenches, hot tea or soup should be ready for the men, and boots, puttees and socks will be removed, and a dry pair of the latter put on before " turning in." Men must rub each other's feet, as a man cannot massage his own feet properly.

(f) An officer will always supervise the rubbing of feet on return from the trenches, and will report that this has been completed before he turns in himself.